PIONEERING NONPROFIT AI INITIATIVES

A Guide to Generational Diversity, Ethics, and Collaboration

AINSLEY K. HINES

A. Kay Publishing LLC

Disclosure Statment

This book, "Pioneering Nonprofit AI Initiatives: A Guide to Generational Diversity, Ethics, and Collaboration," is intended for informational and educational purposes only. It provides insights, recommendations, and perspectives on nonprofit AI initiatives, generational diversity, ethics, and collaboration. The information in this book is based on a collection of publicly available sources, research, expert opinions, and insights generated by the AI model. The author and publisher of this book have made every effort to ensure the accuracy of the information presented. However, it is essential to acknowledge the following:

1. No Legal Advice: This book does not constitute legal, professional, or financial advice. It is separate from professional consultation or guidance. Readers are encouraged to seek the advice of qualified professionals regarding their specific legal or financial situations.

2. Copyright and Fair Use: Certain quotes, excerpts, or references from copyrighted materials are used under "fair use" principles defined by applicable copyright law. The author and publisher have made reasonable efforts to acknowledge and cite sources where appropriate.

3. Liability: The author and publisher are not liable for any potential consequences, damages, or legal actions resulting from using the information in this book. Readers assume full responsibility for their interpretation and application of the content.

4. Accuracy and Timeliness: The information presented in this book is accurate to the best of the author's

knowledge up to the knowledge cutoff date of December 2023. Readers should verify any facts, data, or legal matters discussed in this book to ensure they remain current.

5. Independent Judgment: The guidance and suggestions in this book are provided to assist readers in making informed decisions. Readers need to exercise their independent judgment, consider their unique circumstances, and conduct further research when making decisions related to nonprofit AI initiatives.

By accessing and reading this book, readers agree to the terms of this disclosure statement. The author and publisher disclaim any liability or responsibility for actions taken by readers based on the information presented in this book. If readers have concerns about specific legal or copyright matters, it is advisable to consult with legal or copyright professionals. This disclosure statement is intended to protect both the author and readers and to ensure that the information provided is used responsibly and ethically.

Content

Conclusion

INTRODUCTION

The nonprofit sector comprises a diverse group of generations who come together with a shared goal of positively impacting society. As we explore this connection of generational diversity and AI adoption in nonprofits, we must understand each generation's unique attributes and perspectives. The Silent Generation, Baby Boomers, Generation X, Millennials, and Generation Z all bring distinct strengths and values.

Nonprofits thrive on diversity, and generational diversity is no exception. The Silent Generation, often characterized by their experience and stability, can offer valuable insights and guidance. Baby Boomers are known for their work ethic and commitment to the cause. Generation X bridges the gap between traditional and modern approaches, while Millennials bring innovation, tech-savviness, and a passion for social change. The emerging Generation Z offers fresh insights and a deep understanding of digital communication.

AI technologies can enhance efficiency, decision-making, and impact in the nonprofit sector. AI offers many opportunities to drive positive change, from predictive analytics to automated donor engagement. However, as technology increasingly intertwines with the nonprofit sector, understanding how each generation perceives and engages with AI is crucial. Diversity is often touted as a cornerstone of innovation. Studies have shown that diverse teams tend to be more creative, adaptable, and effective in problem-solving (Cox, 1994; Page, 2007). The fusion of generational diversity and AI in nonprofits has the potential to create a powerful synergy. Different generations bring their unique approaches, experiences, and insights to the table, making the integration of AI more holistic.

We shall explore the nuances of each generation's relationship with AI, discover ways to tailor AI adoption to their needs, and ultimately leverage this diversity to drive positive change. Understanding how each generation perceives and engages with AI can ensure that AI adoption is inclusive and effective for all generations involved in nonprofit organizations. In a world where data is abundant, AI can benefit nonprofit organizations by helping them make sense of it, leading to more informed decisions and resource allocation. AI can also streamline administrative tasks, allowing nonprofit professionals to focus on strategic planning and mission-critical activities. Additionally, AI can enhance donor relationships and facilitate better communication with beneficiaries.

As technology increasingly intertwines with the nonprofit sector, understanding how each generation perceives and engages with AI is crucial. While Diversity and AI form a Winning Combination, Diversity is often touted as a cornerstone of innovation. Studies have shown that diverse teams are more creative, adaptable, and effective in problem-solving. The fusion of generational diversity and AI in nonprofits has the potential to create a powerful synergy. Different generations bring their unique approaches, experiences, and insights to the table, making the integration of AI more holistic.

This book explores the practical steps, strategies, and considerations for successfully integrating AI into nonprofit organizations. It delves into the nuances of each generation's relationship with AI, discovering ways to tailor AI adoption to their needs and leveraging this diversity as a driving force behind positive change. It also explores technological adaptability and resilience and how nonprofit organizations embracing AI must equip themselves to respond swiftly to change and uncertainty. Cross-generational mentorship will be a cornerstone in building adaptability and resilience within organizations. Additionally, ensuring the privacy and security of beneficiary information is paramount in an age where data is a precious commodity. The practices of data privacy, compliance with data protection regulations, data minimization, and anonymization will be illuminated to protect the trust placed in nonprofit organizations.

While not undermining the Ever-Present Generational Diversity, this book reveals how generational perspectives are pivotal in shaping how AI is embraced, adapted, and integrated into nonprofit organizations. Each generation's unique strengths and attributes will become evident, influencing the path forward and shaping the collaborative nature of nonprofit AI initiatives. The theme of cross-generational mentorship will also become integral to our journey, bridging divides and fostering mutual growth.

This book is a comprehensive guide to the world of nonprofit AI initiatives. By understanding the intricacies of generational diversity, embracing ethics and data privacy, nurturing adaptability and resilience, and fostering collaboration, nonprofit organizations can unlock the full potential of AI technology to drive positive social and environmental change. As we navigate these chapters together, you will discover a treasure trove of insights, strategies, and practical steps related to these core themes. Our journey has just begun, and we will explore the intricate and rewarding terrain of nonprofit AI initiatives.

PART ONE:

THE NONPROFIT ECOSYSTEM

CHAPTER ONE

The Advent of Nonprofit Organizations

Overview of Nonprofit Organization

A Nonprofit Organization (NPO) is a legal entity that operates to achieve a social or public benefit rather than generating profits for its owners or shareholders. Unlike for-profit organizations that exist to make a financial gain, nonprofit organizations are dedicated to pursuing their mission-oriented goals through the collective actions of citizens.

The primary focus of nonprofit organizations is to serve a community's collective needs and address social issues that the government or private sector may need to address adequately. They may provide various services such as education, healthcare, social welfare, environmental conservation, or cultural preservation. Non-profit organizations may also advocate and lobby to promote policies and laws aligning with their mission.

Nonprofit organizations, such as corporations, trusts, foundations, or associations, can take various legal forms. They are typically tax-exempt under the applicable laws, which means they do not have to pay income taxes on their earnings as long as they use these funds to further their charitable purposes. This tax exemption allows non-profit organizations to allocate more resources to their programs and services instead of paying taxes.

The IRS federal code—501 (c)(3) made provisions for the

following:
- It allows NPOs to receive tax-deductible donations.
- It guarantees eligibility for grants.
- It helps build credibility.

To obtain this tax-exempt status from the Internal Revenue Service (IRS), nonprofit organizations (NPOs) must demonstrate that they serve a social cause and provide a public benefit. This status allows individuals and businesses to deduct their taxes from their earnings, while the NPO itself does not have to pay taxes on donations or revenues from fundraising activities; nevertheless, NPOs cannot be politically affiliated, as this helps maintain a non-partisan tone in their communications.

Attributes of Nonprofit Organization

Non-profit organizations are governed by a board of directors or trustees responsible for overseeing their operations and ensuring they remain true to their mission and values. They are accountable to their stakeholders, including donors, beneficiaries, and regulatory agencies, and must adhere to strict financial reporting and transparency standards.

Charitable nonprofits are a vital component of American society. They serve as a means for individuals to collaborate towards a common goal and bring together their shared values and aspirations to life. These organizations feed, care for, shelter, educate, inspire, enlighten, and nurture people of all backgrounds and demographics. They also foster civic engagement and leadership, promoting economic growth and strengthening the fabric of communities.

Indeed, nonprofit organizations serve crucial societal roles by addressing critical issues, promoting social justice, and providing essential services. These are evident in areas of charities by offering direct assistance to individuals in need; in social service agencies by supporting vulnerable populations; through advocacy by raising awareness on social issues; through educational institutions by providing education, training, and research institutions; Museums and art galleries are not left behind as they preserve cultural heritage; through sports organizations by promoting physical activity, as well as through religious organizations, offering spiritual guidance.

While nonprofits can generate profits, they cannot distribute them to private individuals. This restriction against "private benefit" is because tax-exempt charitable nonprofits exist to serve the public interest, not personal interests. Foundation grants represent only a tiny portion of the total amount of money contributed annually to the charitable nonprofit community, while private philanthropy, which includes donations from individuals and grants from private and corporate foundations, accounts for only 14% of the total annual revenue for the charitable nonprofit sector, with the majority coming from individual contributions.

All charitable nonprofits benefit from public support and donations, relying heavily on private donations to serve their communities. While individual taxpayers receive only a partial tax benefit for charitable contributions, the community served by the charitable nonprofit gets the total value of every dollar contributed.

Challenges of Nonprofit Organization

As laudable as nonprofit initiatives are, they also experience significant challenges that may hinder their ability to serve the communities they serve optimally. Many of these challenges are systemic, affecting the whole sector, and can be internal or external.

Internal challenges include issues related to governance, personnel, and financial accountability. Governance can be in the overall management and decision-making processes within an organization. Personnel challenges can arise due to a lack of skilled staff or high turnover rates, negatively impacting the organization's operations and effectiveness. Financial accountability can ensure that funds are used appropriately and efficiently for the intended purposes. It is, therefore, imperative for nonprofits to maintain financial transparency and adhere to strict financial reporting standards.

On the other hand are external challenges, which include fundraising and operational issues that are systemic and sector-wide. Fundraising challenges may include increasing donor competition, declining government funding, and changing donors' preferences. Operational challenges include rising costs of goods and services, increasing regulatory requirements, and growing competition from for-profit organizations.

Nonprofits can overcome these obstacles by fostering collaboration and cooperation among organizations. Collaboration can lead to more significant achievements than working independently due to the opportunity to share resources, expertise, and knowledge.

CHAPTER TWO

Nonprofit Initiatives and Values

Nonprofit Initiatives

Nonprofit initiatives are the projects or programs undertaken by nonprofit organizations typically addressing social or environmental issues. These initiatives can vary in size and scope. Still, they often involve mobilizing resources and volunteers to carry out specific activities, such as fundraising for a cause or creating awareness about social issues.

Nonprofits launch new initiatives for various reasons. One of the primary motivations is to make a difference in their communities by addressing pressing social issues. For instance, a nonprofit may launch an initiative to combat homelessness, provide affordable housing, or address food insecurity in the community.

Another reason may be to provide much-needed assistance to needy people, particularly during times of crisis, such as natural disasters. Such initiatives may provide affected communities with emergency relief, shelter, and necessities.

Nonprofits also launch initiatives to raise awareness about social issues that are often overlooked or underreported. For example, a nonprofit may launch an initiative to combat animal cruelty, promote women's rights, or address mental health and well-being issues.

Additionally, nonprofits may launch initiatives to inspire others to take action, often involving community outreach programs, training sessions, and workshops to empower individuals and communities to take ownership of social issues and work towards solutions.

Lastly, NPOs may launch initiatives to build relationships with other community members and local organizations such as businesses, government agencies, and foundations. Such initiatives often involve partnerships and collaborations to leverage resources and expertise to achieve shared goals and objectives.

Non-Profit Values

Value is defined as the guiding principles and beliefs of people or organizations through their daily activities. For nonprofits, values are the fundamental principles that underpin the actions, decisions, and conduct of nonprofit organizations. These values serve as a guiding force for nonprofits, helping them make decisions and choices. They define the character and culture of the NPOs while providing a compass for its members to follow, often rooted in a commitment to social justice, equality, and service to others, focusing on transparency, accountability, and collaboration.

Some common nonprofit values include:
1. **Service:** Nonprofits are committed to serving others and making a positive difference. This is the value at the heart of all nonprofits.
2. **Social Justice**: Nonprofits promote social justice and address societal systemic inequalities.
3. **Collaboration:** Their various partnerships and shared resources reflect the importance of working with other organizations and stakeholders to achieve shared goals.
4. **Transparency:** Nonprofits are committed to being open and honest about their operations, finances, and impact. This is reflected in their efforts to provide regular reports,

engage in dialogue with stakeholders, and adhere to rigorous standards of financial accountability.

5. **Accountability:** Nonprofits take responsibility for their actions and decisions, recognizing that they must act in the best interests of their beneficiaries and stakeholders.

Importance of Nonprofit Values

Some of the values of NPOs are:
1. It provides a sense of purpose and direction for NPOs by guiding them to stay focused and accurate to their goals and mission.
2. It builds trust and credibility. When individuals and organizations act by their values, they build trust and credibility with their stakeholders.
3. It promotes social cohesion by providing a shared set of beliefs and ideals that unite individuals and organizations, fostering community and solidarity.
4. It facilitates decision-making by providing a framework for evaluating options and making choices.

CHAPTER THREE

Leadership Approach for Nonprofits

T he strength of any organization lies in its leadership's effectiveness, which is particularly true for non-profit organizations (NPOs) because their leadership differs from conventional business leadership, given their unique objectives and focal points. To successfully navigate the intricacies of nonprofit work, one must have a leadership style tailored to connect various elements.

Elements of Effective Leadership for Nonprofits:
1. Data and Results-oriented: One of the interests of nonprofit leaders is achieving measurable results that positively impact the community. They set clear goals and objectives, and they can measure and report on their progress towards these goals.
2. Collaborative: NPO leaders know the importance of collaborating with stakeholders, including beneficiaries, donors, partners, and staff. Hence, they maintain strong relationships based on trust and respect while receiving input and feedback from all stakeholders.
3. Mission-driven: Leaders of NPOs prioritize the organization's mission above everything else. They ensure that all activities and decisions align with the mission and

values of the organization.

4.   Strategic: Nonprofit leaders have a clear vision for the organization and can articulate it; they can also develop and implement effective strategies aligning with its mission and values.

5.   Adaptable: Nonprofit leaders are flexible and willing to take calculated risks to pursue their mission. This is evident in their ability to adapt to changing circumstances and respond to new opportunities and challenges.

6.   Transparent and Ethical: NPO leaders prioritize transparency in operations, finances, and decision-making processes. They are open and honest with stakeholders about the organization's activities, challenges, and successes.

7.   Learning-oriented: Nonprofit leaders prioritize continuous improvement in all aspects of their work by investing in professional development for themselves and their staff, and they are committed to staying up-to-date on best practices in their field.

Leadership Styles for Nonprofit

Nonprofit leadership styles can vary, but all influential leaders share specific core characteristics. The best leadership style for an NPO will be determined by its particular objectives and vision.

1.   **Transformational leadership**: From a passionate, optimistic, and confident standpoint. It embodies the organization's values and uses the nonprofit's vision to motivate all aspects of its work while inspiring others to share their enthusiasm to serve its mission.

2.   **Charismatic leadership**: NPO leaders who adopt a charismatic style have engaging personalities that foster enthusiasm for the nonprofit's activities and mission. They communicate well and can persuade others to follow their vision while taking risks that can either pay off or challenge the organization's sustainability.

3. **Transactional leadership:** This leadership style adopts a transactional style using goal setting as a motivational tool. Success is defined as meeting established goals, and may need more forward-thinking skills if innovation interferes with their goals. They can be effective fundraisers and meet financial goals even when others fail.

4. **Participative leadership:** Nonprofit leaders who adopt a participative style believe collaboration is critical to the organization's success. They listen to their team members and stakeholders, delegate tasks, and promote collaboration

5. **Servant leadership:** This is a form of leadership where the well-being of others is prioritized, and power is shared as a form of motivation. They work to help others find success both as people and as professionals.

The Power of Collaboration

Working collaboratively is essential for the success of NPOs. Nonprofits may encounter challenges because they need more resources to deal with complex problems. However, when they collaborate, they can achieve great results. Collaboration can also lead to increased accountability and transparency in nonprofit organizations. By working with other organizations and stakeholders, nonprofit leaders can be held more accountable for their actions and decisions. Collaborative efforts also promote efficient use of resources, new ideas, best practices, and lasting success.

Working collaboratively is essential for the success of NPOs. Nonprofits may encounter challenges because they need more resources to deal with complex problems. However, when they collaborate, they can achieve great results. Collaboration can also lead to increased accountability and transparency in nonprofit organizations. By working with other organizations and stakeholders, nonprofit leaders can be held more accountable for their actions and decisions. Collaborative efforts also promote efficient use of resources, new ideas, best practices, and lasting success.

Types of Collaboration

1. Joint Ventures are when two or more NPOs collaborate and work on a particular project or idea.
2. Partnerships are when NPOs use their combined skills and resources with businesses, government groups, or other organizations.
3. Networks: This is an informal group of non-profits that share information, resources, and best practices.

PART TWO:

ARTIFICIAL INTELLIGENCE (AI)

CHAPTER FOUR

Emergence of Artificial Intelligence

A rtificial intelligence (AI) is a branch of computer science that focuses on creating intelligent systems, also known as agents, that can think, learn, and act independently. Essentially, AI aims to make machines as intelligent as humans to perform tasks requiring intelligence.

Artificial Intelligence (AI) is not just about making machines act like humans. It is about creating a new kind of intelligence that can think, learn, and interact with the world in ways that were once only possible for humans. This idea started with a question from John McCarthy in the 1950s: "Can machines think?" Alan Turing, a visionary mathematician, then suggested that machines could learn from experience, paving the way for AI's evolution (Copeland, 2023). From playing chess to transforming our daily experiences, AI has come a long way in over six decades.

AI has many applications in healthcare, finance, transportation, and manufacturing. AI develops new diagnostic tools and treatments in healthcare and provides personalized care. AI is employed in finance to detect fraud, manage risk, and make investment decisions. AI is being utilized in transportation to develop self-driving cars and trucks and optimize traffic flow. In manufacturing, AI is used to automate tasks and enhance product quality (Holt, n.d.). Additionally, AI is used in nonprofit organizations to address social and environmental issues, which will be discussed extensively in the coming chapters. These are just a few examples of how AI is being applied today.

There are different types of AI; two popular ones are machine learning and deep learning. Machine learning lets computers learn and improve without being explicitly programmed, using algorithms and large amounts of data. Deep learning is a type of machine learning that uses artificial neural networks to learn from data and make predictions or decisions. Another type of AI is natural language processing, which allows computers to understand and generate human language, and computer vision, which enables computers to interpret visual information. These are just a few examples of the many types of AI that exist today, and as the field continues to advance, we can expect to see more sophisticated forms of AI in the future.

Characteristics of Artificial Intelligence

AI systems have several essential characteristics. Some of these are highlighted below:

i.   One of the most significant is their ability to learn from data and experience. This ability allows AI to improve its performance over time, as humans do.

ii.   Another critical characteristic is problem-solving. AI systems can tackle complex problems that would be difficult or impossible for humans to solve. They can analyze large amounts of data, identify patterns, and make predictions or recommendations based on their analysis.

iii.   AI systems can also reason about the world around them. They can process information, draw conclusions, and decide based on their reasoning. This is a critical aspect of intelligence, as it allows AI systems to respond to new situations and environments flexibly and adaptively.

iv.   Finally, AI systems are adaptable. This is essential for AI systems to be effective in real-world applications, where they will encounter various situations and environments.

These characteristics make AI systems potent and versatile tools for various applications, from healthcare and finance to transportation, manufacturing, and nonprofits.

CHAPTER FIVE

*Understanding Generational
Differences*

Generational differences refer to different age groups' distinct characteristics, values, and behaviors arising from historical events, technological advancements, socioeconomic factors, and parental influence. Understanding these generational differences is essential for organizations because it allows them to tailor their strategies better to appeal to each generation's unique perspectives and skills. By recognizing the strengths of each generation, organizations can leverage their collective talents to maximize productivity and achieve their goals.

To navigate the complexities of generational differences in the nonprofit sector, it is crucial to understand the unique characteristics, values, and attributes of each generation actively contributing to these organizations. Here is a brief overview:

The Generations in the Workforce

1.   The Silent Generation (born between 1928 and 1945): This generation brings a wealth of experience, stability, and wisdom to nonprofit organizations. Known for their commitment to organizational values and dedication to

causes, they often serve as stalwart leaders and mentors.

2. Baby Boomers (born between 1946 and 1964): Born during a time of significant social and political change, they are known for their work ethic, passion for social causes, and willingness to commit to long-term goals. Their leadership roles are crucial in the nonprofit sector.

3. Generation X (born between 1965 and 1980): Bridging traditional and modern approaches, Generation X values independence, adaptability, and pragmatism. Their influence is pivotal for introducing innovative strategies to help nonprofit organizations stay relevant in an ever-changing landscape.

4. Millennials (Generation Y) (born between 1981 and 1996): Millennials bring fresh perspectives, tech-savviness, and a commitment to social change to nonprofit organizations. They are often catalysts for innovation and digital transformation, helping these organizations stay ahead of the curve.

5. Generation Z (emerging between 1997 and the early 2010s): With a deep understanding of digital communication and a unique social-issue perspective, Generation Z offers new insights and energy to nonprofit organizations as they enter the workforce. Their entry into the workforce brings fresh perspectives that can help these organizations stay relevant in an increasingly digital world.

Perceived Areas of Generational Differences

Generational differences can be observed in various aspects of life, including work ethic, communication preferences, and social values. Baby Boomers, who grew up during economic hardship and war, value hard work and dedication in the workplace. In contrast, Millennials, who have witnessed the rise of technology and globalization, place a greater emphasis on flexibility and purpose in their careers. They seek opportunities for professional development and are more likely to switch jobs in pursuit of their goals.

Communication preferences also vary across generations. Older generations often prefer face-to-face communication, as they grew up when phone calls and letters were the primary modes of communication. Baby Boomers and Traditionalists may prefer traditional forms of communication, such as email or phone calls. At the same time, younger generations are more comfortable with digital tools like social media and instant messaging.

Authority is another area where generational differences can be observed. Traditionalists respect authority figures and follow established norms and hierarchies. Baby Boomers also value authority but are more likely to question authority when they believe it is necessary. Gen X and Y, on the other hand, are more likely to challenge established norms and hierarchies. They value collaboration and teamwork over traditional forms of authority.

Social values also differ across generations. Baby Boomers prioritize personal achievement and financial success. They grew up when these values were highly valued in society. Millennials and Gen Z, however, emphasize social justice and environmental consciousness more. They are more likely to prioritize causes they believe in over personal gain.

Leveraging Each Generation's Strengths
Every generation has something valuable to offer, and recognizing these strengths can lead to effective collaboration and synergy.
1.   Leveraging the Wisdom of the Silent Generation: The Silent Generation can serve as mentors and advisors, providing historical context and a steady hand in decision-making processes.
2.   Harnessing Baby Boomers' Commitment: Their dedication to causes makes them ideal leaders in the nonprofit sector. Their ability to connect with donors and set long-term strategic goals is invaluable.

3. Adapting with Generation X: Generation X is adaptable and can bridge the gap between traditional and modern approaches. They excel in project management and overseeing complex initiatives.

4. Innovating with Millennials: The Millennials bring innovation and tech-savviness. They can drive digital transformation, enhance donor engagement, and provide fresh insights for the organization.

5. Energizing with Generation Z: The emerging Generation Z offers new perspectives and a deep understanding of digital communication. Their enthusiasm can invigorate nonprofit efforts.

CHAPTER SIX

Artificial Intelligence
Across Generations

Gen Zs are tech-savvy and cautious about AI, using it for social good and creative expression while raising concerns about privacy, bias, and ethical implications. Millennials are skeptical but curious, aware of AI's potential benefits and drawbacks. Gen X is adapting and embracing AI tools that enhance productivity and personal life, valuing human-centric AI. Baby Boomers, however, are learning new skills to integrate AI into their lives, with some hesitant but many actively seeking its applications.

The Power of Intergenerational Collaboration

In the fast-evolving world of nonprofit organizations, intergenerational collaboration can be a game-changer for innovation and progress. Each generation brings unique perspectives, skills, and experiences to the table, and harnessing their collective strengths can lead to more effective running of nonprofits.

To achieve this, it is essential to understand the benefits and strategies of intergenerational collaboration. Firstly, unlocking the potential of intergenerational collaboration involves recognizing that each generation has something valuable to offer.

Gen Zs are tech-savvy and adept at using AI tools but also have concerns about privacy, bias, and ethical implications. Millennials are skeptical but curious about AI and aware of its potential benefits and drawbacks. Generation X is adapting and embracing AI tools that enhance productivity and personal life, valuing human-centric AI that complements human capabilities without replacing them. Baby Boomers are learning new skills to integrate AI into their lives, with some hesitant but many actively seeking its applications.

Secondly, bridging the generational gap involves finding common ground and addressing differences. This can be achieved by fostering open communication, respecting each other's perspectives, and finding ways to leverage each other's strengths. For example, Gen Zs can bring fresh ideas and a deep understanding of emerging technologies, while Baby Boomers can bring wisdom and experience gained over a lifetime of service.

Thirdly, harmonizing generational values with AI initiatives ensures that AI is developed responsibly and inclusively. This means addressing concerns about privacy, bias, and ethical implications head-on and involving all generations in decision-making. Gen Zs are particularly interested in using AI for social good and creative expression while advocating for responsible development and inclusivity.

Lastly, celebrating collaborative success involves recognizing the achievements of intergenerational teams and sharing them widely. This can help to build momentum for intergenerational collaboration within nonprofit organizations and inspire others to follow suit. Nonprofit organizations can achieve more significant innovation, progress, and impact by unlocking the potential of intergenerational cooperation, bridging the generational gap, harmonizing generational values with AI initiatives, and celebrating collaborative success.

The Importance of Collaboration in AI Initiatives

1. Leveraging Diverse Expertise: Collaboration between individuals with diverse expertise can lead to cross-disciplinary innovation and drive AI initiatives that align with nonprofit missions. By leveraging each generation's unique perspectives and skills, nonprofits can harness the collective strengths of their teams to address complex challenges. Practical strategies for nonprofits include engaging staff members of different generations in discussions about collaboration in AI projects, encouraging them to share insights on how diverse teams can benefit AI initiatives, and fostering open communication, respect for each other's perspectives, and a focus on responsible and inclusive AI development.

2. Strengthening Impact: Nonprofits can strengthen their impact by working together to address complex social and environmental challenges more effectively. Strategies to achieve this include collaborating with staff members from diverse generations to identify opportunities for expanding the collaborative nature of AI projects and developing a culture emphasizing the shared mission and the strength of working together. By doing so, nonprofits can maximize the potential of AI to create positive change in the communities they serve.

3. Generational Attitudes toward Teamwork: Different generations may have distinct attitudes towards teamwork and collaboration. While younger generations may be more receptive to collaborative efforts, older generations may prioritize individual expertise. Nonprofits can foster discussions that explore these generational attitudes and encourage open dialogue that considers the experiences and perspectives of each generation. By understanding these attitudes, nonprofits can develop a collaboration strategy that resonates with the values and concerns of all ages, promoting intergenerational collaboration and teamwork.

4. Cross-Generational Mentorship: This can facilitate the

transfer of collaborative skills and teamwork values. Older generations can mentor younger generations in effective collaboration, while younger generations can share insights into leveraging technology for collaboration.

5. Creating cross-generational teams that work together on AI initiatives can promote collaboration and shared ownership of projects. Nonprofits can assign leaders from different generations to facilitate communication and cooperation among team members. This can be achieved by collaborating with team members from different generations to establish cross-generational project teams, creating a culture that values each generation's diverse strengths, and promoting open communication and respect for each other's perspectives.

6. Investing in collaboration tools and technology that facilitate communication and knowledge sharing ensures that everyone can use the tools to collaborate and share knowledge, promoting intergenerational collaboration and collaboration across disciplines. These tools should be user-friendly and meet the needs of staff members of all ages.

7. Highlighting and recognizing collaborative leaders through awards, public acknowledgments, or other forms of recognition and sharing their stories as part of the organization's communication strategy as examples of the organization's commitment to teamwork can inspire others to follow suit and contribute to the success of AI projects. By doing so, nonprofits can reinforce the importance of collaboration and encourage others to adopt collaborative practices in their work.

PART THREE:

ARTIFICIAL INTELLIGENCE (AI)
AND NONPROFIT INITIATIVES

CHAPTER SEVEN

Embracing Technological Changes
within Nonprofit Organizations

I n the nonprofit sector, time and money are crucial components of fundraising efforts and achieving key goals, and as a nonprofit professional, maximizing both assets is a top priority. Artificial intelligence (AI) has gained significant attention in the nonprofit sector, with AI and machine learning for nonprofits being a trending topic for quite some time now.

Previously, AI technology was out of reach for many nonprofits with limited budgets or tech capacities. Today, organizations of all shapes and sizes can use AI to fundraise smarter and more efficiently. As time and money remain scarce in the nonprofit sector, AI presents an exciting opportunity for organizations to maximize their impact while minimizing costs.

While AI-driven fundraising is the next major trend for forward-thinking nonprofits. AI tools can also automate tasks, generate financial reports, and create customer databases to track donor engagement and analyze donor data. They can also lay the groundwork for crafting a nonprofit mission and establishing guidelines for team members and stakeholders.

The proliferation of AI tools presents an opportunity for

nonprofits to leverage these technologies to their advantage. AI can save nonprofit professionals valuable time and money performing everyday tasks, research, and processes. The advent of the COVID-19 pandemic, by imperative, necessitated nonprofits to use their data in more innovative ways than ever before, which means AI solutions are becoming increasingly important.

However, while more nonprofits realize the immense value of collecting data to guide their strategies, only some have the time, resources, and expertise to generate value with that data. The range of AI solutions is vast; the right tool, therefore, depends on what is needed. Nonprofits can choose from simple solutions that solve one specific pain point for their target audience or complete software management tools that streamline all workflows.

AI is revolutionizing how nonprofits operate by enabling them to work more efficiently without compromising on resources by empowering them to maximize their resources and discover innovative ways to engage donors. The potential of AI for nonprofits lies in its ability to supplement the two resources that most fundraising organizations need: more time and money.

However, the success of AI for nonprofits depends on using the right tools and providing them with quality data. With an overwhelming number of AI products flooding the market, it is crucial to experiment and identify the tools that best suit your organization's requirements. By leveraging AI tools, nonprofits can optimize their operations, freeing time to focus on building and maintaining relationships with their supporters and beneficiaries. This remains a critical aspect of nonprofit work that requires a human touch.

Adopting AI in Nonprofit

AI offers numerous applications, particularly for nonprofit organizations, and as AI becomes more prevalent in society, the possibilities for how organizations can utilize it for their benefit are hereunder listed:

1.   Donor Analysis:

AI tools can analyze donor, external wealth, and philanthropic data to predict and recommend donors who will most likely give when, how frequently, how much they will provide, and the best approach for reaching out to them. It can also screen prospective donors, segment audiences, and create predictive models about their behavior. By inputting data about past and potential donors, nonprofits can identify new donor sources and offer suggestions on how to engage them. This information helps nonprofits tailor their outreach work to each individual, leading to not just securing one donation but building lasting relationships that result in continued giving and engagement.

2.   Manage Administrative and Routine Tasks

Managing administrative and routine tasks in the nonprofit sector can significantly burden staff resources. However, the implementation of AI technology can help alleviate these challenges. AI can perform various time-consuming, expensive functions prone to human error, such as collecting and analyzing data, reviewing and updating donor prospect profiles, reading and responding to incoming communications, scheduling meetings, and sending internal and external reminders. By automating these tasks, AI can free up staff time to focus on more critical work and reduce the risk of human error. This is particularly essential for data-driven fundraising that relies on accurate information.

3.   Social Media Engagement

In today's digital age, social media has become a powerful tool for nonprofit organizations to engage with their supporters, promote their fundraising campaigns, and share updates about their mission. With the influence of AI, social media platforms are now using AI algorithms to make charitable giving recommendations to users, making it easier for nonprofits to reach potential donors.

Nonprofits can use AI-powered social media management tools to maximize the impact of social media for fundraising.

These tools can help analyze social media trends, make content recommendations, write posts, text, image captions, and hashtags, schedule posts, recycle content, and monitor engagement on multiple platforms. Using these tools, nonprofits can create effective call-to-actions that drive traffic to online donation pages and monitor other fundraising organizations' actions.

4.   Manage volunteers

Nonprofits can enhance their volunteer management processes with AI technology by finding high-quality volunteers, providing personalized training based on each volunteer's skills and experience, creating dynamic scheduling systems, facilitating communication, managing expenses, collecting feedback, and writing customized appreciation notes for their hard work. By leveraging AI technology, nonprofits can optimize their volunteer management processes, resulting in a more engaged and effective volunteer base better aligned with their mission and values.

5.   Chatbots Assistants

Powered by artificial intelligence, Chatbots can serve as friendly and conversational assistants on a nonprofit's website, providing prompt and personalized customer service to anyone who visits the site. These AI-driven bots can answer common questions, offer assistance, and even encourage donations at any time of day, as they operate 24/7. Whether a donor is enquiring about making a contribution or a beneficiary seeking guidance on accessing services, chatbots are always available to provide quick, round-the-clock support to enhance the overall user experience for visitors.

6.   Event Planning / Management

Nonprofit organizations can significantly enhance their event planning processes using artificial intelligence (AI) technology. AI can assist in identifying the most optimal dates, times, venues, topics, and speakers for an event based on various factors such as location, capacity, amenities, and costs. AI can also streamline registration and ticketing processes for a smoother user experience. AI can translate languages and upraise e-events during the event while creating tailored experiences and obtaining feedback. By leveraging AI technology in event planning, nonprofits can create memorable experiences that attract more support for their mission and bring their entire community closer together.

7.   Data Management

Nonprofit organizations can simplify their data management processes using AI technology. AI can clean and organize datasets, integrate data from multiple sources, detect security threats, and generate data visualizations. As the organization grows, managing data at scale becomes crucial, and AI tools can make the process more manageable. By leveraging AI technology for data management, nonprofits can make informed decisions based on accurate and usable data.

8.   Fraud detection

Nonprofit organizations can simplify fraud detection using artificial intelligence (AI) technology. AI algorithms can analyze financial transactions, donations, and grant distributions to identify any deviations from the norm, which could indicate fraud. This technology allows nonprofits to detect potential fraud quickly and efficiently, enabling them to take prompt action to address any issues. Additionally, AI algorithms trained to understand language can detect suspicious or fraud-indicative language in written communication, such as emails, chat logs, or donation forms.

Examples of AI Tools for Nonprofits

Many AI tools are being used in nonprofits as a potent force to enhance efficiency, engagement, and impact. However, selecting the right AI tool requires careful consideration and experimentation. Here are a few AI tools that can be useful for nonprofit organizations:

1.   **DonorSearch AI**: This tool uses intelligent algorithms to

connect donors with the causes they care about, making fundraising more successful.

2.   **VolunteerMatch:** This platform matches volunteers with opportunities that suit their skills and interests, using AI to connect them with organizations based on location, skills, and availability. This enhances volunteer satisfaction and retention.

3.   **Sisense:** This robust analytics platform lets you extract valuable insights from your data without requiring coding experience. It aids in analyzing donor data to inform your fundraising strategies. Predictive analytics, which employs statistics and modeling techniques, is utilized to foresee future outcomes.

4.   **Otter.ai:** serves as an AI meeting assistant, recording audio, transcribing speech into text, capturing slides, and providing real-time summaries. It seamlessly integrates with your Google or Microsoft calendar and can automatically join and record Zoom, Microsoft Teams, and Google Meet meetings.

5.   **Fathom:** is an AI tool for meeting minutes that automatically records, transcribes, and summarizes critical discussions. It works well with Zoom and connects to other platforms like Slack, Salesforce, and Hubspot. This allows you to access all your meeting records in one place, making it easy to keep track of critical action items.

6.   **AdCopy:** works as a virtual marketing assistant that can create, rewrite, and optimize ads using just a link, a logo, and a few prompts. It offers customization options that sync with Meta Ads Manager data and testing to produce ads that are effective in getting results.

7.   **Buffer:** This social media management tool offers features to suggest content ideas, repurpose posts, and condense long content into shorter ones. It can also find trending

topics, current events, seasonal ideas, and more to create engaging posts that go viral and connect with audiences.

8.   **Tango**: is a guide generator that turns any process into a step-by-step interactive guide. Easily share these guides with staff and volunteers, and use shared insights to measure, optimize, and collaborate on ideas for effective results.

9.   **TARS:** is a chatbot platform that enhances a donor's customer experience through engaging and intuitive interactions. Its no-code builder facilitates interactions between nonprofits and potential donors, guiding them through the donation process.

10.   **ManyChat:** is a chat marketing tool that can help nonprofits boost conversions on platforms like Instagram, WhatsApp, and Messenger. Connect instantly with potential donors to address fundamental questions, respond to social media comments, and automate FAQs to guide them through the donation process.

Navigating the AI Landscape: Tips for Nonprofits

1.   **Selecting the Right AI**
   - Align with purpose: Before diving in, define your goals and values. Choose AI tools that complement your mission and enhance your impact, not drive it.
   - Seek diverse options: The AI landscape is vast! Research and compare various platforms, considering their strengths, weaknesses, and cost-effectiveness. Remember, there is no one-size-fits-all solution.
   - Start small, scale smart: Do not get overwhelmed. Begin with one or two AI tools that address specific needs and gradually expand as comfort and expertise grow.

2.   **Building Your Team – Intergenerational Collaboration**
   - Embrace diversity: Assemble a team with varied

backgrounds and perspectives. This fosters a critical lens for identifying potential biases in AI algorithms and ensures equitable outcomes for all stakeholders.

- Invest in training: Equip your team with the knowledge and skills to effectively understand, implement, and manage AI.
- Foster collaboration: Create a culture where open communication and feedback are encouraged. This allows for continuous learning and adaptation of your AI initiatives.

3. **Continuity and Evaluation**

- Monitor and evaluate: Regularly assess the impact of your AI tools. Track their effectiveness in achieving your goals, identify areas for improvement, and adapt your strategies accordingly.
- Transparency and trust: Be transparent about collecting, using, and protecting data. Transparency fosters trust with stakeholders and ensures responsible AI practices.
- Accountability and impact: Establish clear accountability structures to address any unintended consequences of your AI initiatives. Remember, AI is a powerful tool whose impact must be carefully considered.

CHAPTER EIGHT

*Challenges of AI Adoption
for Nonprofits*

Adopting artificial intelligence (AI) by nonprofits presents opportunities for transformation in different areas. However, there are challenges, too. Nevertheless, this technological leap is not without its challenges, some of which are listed below:

1. Availability and Quality of Data

Nonprofits thrive on insights gleaned from data. However, AI models are only as good as the data they are trained on. Inaccurate or insufficient data can lead to biased outcomes, jeopardizing crucial decisions and undermining trust. This challenge can be managed by:

- Investing in data quality: Clean, well-structured, and relevant data is essential. This may involve data cleansing, labeling, and standardization efforts.
- Embrace collaboration: Partner with data scientists and necessary stakeholders to pool resources and access broader datasets.
- Prioritize transparency: Be open about data sources and methodologies used to train AI models.

2. Financial Implication

Implementing AI can be resource-intensive. The initial costs of acquiring and training models and hardware and software needs can seem daunting. However, viewing AI as an investment in long-term efficiency is crucial. Nonprofits can justify the initial investment by:

- Considering Scalability: AI's ability to automate tasks frees up human resources for more impactful work.
- Exploring Donor Acquisition: AI-powered marketing enhances outreach personalization, improving fundraising effectiveness.
- Focusing on Operational Efficiency: Predictive analytics aids in optimizing resource allocation and streamlining operations.
- By focusing on the ROI of AI, nonprofits can justify the initial investment and ensure long-term benefits.

3. Lack of Expertise and Skills

Embracing AI requires a shift in skills and mindsets. Nonprofits may need more internal expertise to manage and utilize AI effectively. This gap can be bridged through:

- Skills Training: Investing in staff training and workshops covering AI fundamentals, ethical considerations, and model interpretation is essential.
- Building Internal Partnerships: Leveraging existing talents within the organization, such as data analysts or IT specialists, can provide crucial support for AI adoption.
- External Partnerships: Collaborating with AI consultancies can help develop customized solutions and build internal capacity.

4.   Ethical and Regulatory Factors:

Data privacy, bias, and transparency are factors that are crucial to the adoption of AI. Nonprofits stepping outside regulatory boundaries invites legal woes, tarnished reputations, and mistrust. Navigating this minefield requires:

- consistent monitoring of evolving regulations

- proactive implementation of safeguards
- collaboration with legal and ethics experts
- responsible data utilization that prioritizes both privacy and fairness.

5. Complexity of the Technological Sphere

Embracing AI demands compatible technological infrastructure and a robust architecture. Consider your existing systems, data pipelines, and computing power needs. Building or adapting your tech framework ensures smooth integration and unleashes the full potential of AI.

6. Security Issues:

While AI boosts efficiency, it also creates openings for malicious influence and data misuse, and as AI is being adopted, prioritizing security becomes pertinent for Nonprofits. Aligning AI with internal policies and company values is crucial. Regular security training for personnel and constant monitoring of existing systems help solidify your defenses and maintain trust.

Measuring and Maximizing the Impact of AI Adoption

In nonprofit organizations, measuring and maximizing the impact of AI adoption is critical to achieving mission-driven goals. This chapter delves into evaluating AI initiatives, setting performance metrics, and leveraging the strengths of different generations to ensure the full realization of AI's potential.

A. Setting and Monitoring AI Performance Metrics

Defining Clear Objectives: The successful adoption of AI hinges on well-defined objectives. Nonprofits should establish measurable goals that align with their mission and leverage the capabilities of AI for maximum impact. Team members should be engaged in goal-setting. Their insights ensure that AI objectives are mission-focused and resonate with the organization's values.

ii.   Data-Driven Evaluation: AI generates vast amounts of data that can be leveraged for evaluation. Data analytics tools can provide insights into the effectiveness of AI initiatives. Ensure that Key Performance Indicators (KPIs) align with the nonprofit's mission and goals. Implement regular data analysis and reporting involving team members with relevant data expertise.

B.   Generational Differences in Measuring Impact

Different generations may have varying perspectives on what constitutes a meaningful impact. Understanding these differences is vital for aligning AI initiatives with the organization's values. This can be achieved by facilitating discussions that explore generational perspectives on impact and encouraging open dialogue that allows each generation to express their views.

C.   Leveraging Generational Strengths in Maximizing Impact

i.   Innovation and Problem-Solving: The collective strengths of different generations can be harnessed to maximize the impact of AI. Younger generations may bring innovative problem-solving skills, while older generations offer wisdom and historical context. An environment where ideas flow freely, and team members feel comfortable sharing their insights should be created, which would encourage cross-generational teams to collaborate on AI projects.

ii.   Mission Alignment: Nonprofits must ensure that the impact of AI initiatives aligns with their mission. Different generations may have varying expectations and understanding of how AI contributes to the task; they should, therefore, be engaged and encouraged to identify how AI initiatives directly contribute to the nonprofit's mission. This collaborative approach ensures that AI projects reflect shared values and goals.

D.   Celebrating Impact and Recognizing Contributions

Acknowledgment of Success: Recognizing and celebrating the impact of AI initiatives is essential for boosting morale and motivation for staff members across generations. An acknowledgment and rewards system should be implemented to celebrate AI-related achievements and teams contributing to the mission-driven impact.

By setting and monitoring performance metrics, understanding generational differences in measuring impact, and leveraging generational strengths, nonprofit organizations can ensure that AI adoption leads to the most significant possible impact, aligned with their mission and values.

CHAPTER NINE

*Building a Sustainable and
Inclusive AI Ecosystem*

Creating and nurturing a sustainable and inclusive AI ecosystem within a nonprofit organization is crucial for its ongoing success; the development and deployment of AI must, therefore, be guided by principles of sustainability and inclusivity. Below are a few reasons why inclusivity matters in AI adoption for nonprofits.

i. Diverse perspectives lead to better solutions: When we bring together people from different backgrounds and experiences, we tap into a broader range of ideas and approaches, leading to more effective and impactful AI solutions for the communities we serve.

ii. Building trust and legitimacy: In a world increasingly wary of technology, ensuring that AI development and deployment reflects the needs and values of diverse communities is crucial for building trust and legitimacy.
iii. Unlocking hidden talent: The nonprofit sector comprises passionate individuals with untapped potential in AI. Creating an inclusive environment can empower everyone to contribute their unique skills and knowledge.

Here are some critical steps to build a thriving AI ecosystem that benefits everyone:

1. Embrace generational diversity:
This can be achieved by bridging the knowledge gap through mentor programs and knowledge-sharing initiatives. This can help younger generations learn from the experience of seasoned professionals, while older generations can benefit from the fresh perspectives and tech-savvy of their younger counterparts. Also, investing in training and development provides opportunities for all staff, regardless of age or background, to acquire the skills and knowledge needed to work effectively with AI.

2. Governance and Regulation:
To ensure the responsible and trustworthy use of artificial intelligence within the nonprofit organization, it is crucial to develop ethical guidelines and frameworks such as transparency, accountability, and privacy protection to guide AI development and deployment. Also, a robust regulatory framework should be initiated to mitigate risks associated with using AI. International cooperation is also necessary to develop and implement standards and regulations that align with global values that promote responsible AI practices.

3. Sustainable Development:
Nonprofit organizations can contribute to sustainable development by implementing AI solutions prioritizing long-term impact on critical global challenges such as climate change, poverty, and healthcare disparities. Additionally, they should focus on resource efficiency by developing energy-efficient AI models and infrastructure that minimize environmental impact. Responsible data collection and use, focusing on privacy, ethics, and avoiding data bias, is also crucial. By adhering to these principles, nonprofits can leverage AI for positive social and environmental outcomes while minimizing negative impacts.

4. Inclusive Access and Participation

This involves bridging the digital divide by investing in infrastructure and training to ensure everyone can access AI tools and resources. It also empowers diverse voices by encouraging participation from underrepresented communities in AI development, research, and decision-making. To address bias and discrimination, AI systems should actively combat algorithmic bias and discrimination to ensure fair and equitable outcomes for all. Using diverse datasets to train AI models can also help avoid perpetuating bias and prejudice. Promoting transparency and accountability by being transparent about how AI is used within the organization and holding oneself accountable for unintended consequences is also crucial.

5.   Investing in Education and Training:

To ensure responsible AI development and use, it is essential to develop AI literacy programs that provide everyone with the skills and knowledge to understand and utilize AI via reskilling and upskilling of the nonprofit workforce. Promoting ethical AI education by integrating ethical considerations into AI education and training programs is also crucial to fostering responsible AI development and use. These efforts will help individuals adapt to the changing job landscape, promote responsible AI practices, and maximize the benefits of AI while minimizing its potential risks.

Ethical Considerations for Nonprofit AI Initiatives

1.   Data Privacy and Security:

Data privacy and security are crucial ethical concerns for nonprofits. As AI increasingly integrates into decision-making processes, sensitive data such as donor information and beneficiary details become essential inputs. To address these concerns, NPOs must adopt stringent measures to ensure data privacy and security. This includes implementing robust security protocols to protect sensitive data from unauthorized access and misuse and being transparent about data collection, use, and storage. NPOs should also obtain informed consent from individuals regarding how their data will be used. By prioritizing data privacy and security, NPOs can build and maintain trust with stakeholders while maximizing the benefits of AI.

2.   Transparency and Accountability:

Non-profit organizations implementing AI should prioritize transparency and accountability in their practices. They should be able to clearly explain how AI decisions are made, particularly when those decisions directly impact individuals or communities. Communication about the use of AI, including its limitations and potential biases, is crucial to maintaining the trust of donors, beneficiaries, and the public. Board members must understand how their organization uses AI and be accountable for its outcomes. Donors, volunteers, vendors, and funders should also be informed about AI usage and goals. Transparency around AI helps build trust with stakeholders that AI is being used ethically in the organization. NPOs should communicate how and why they are using AI and what data they are collecting and using, and be able to explain their AI models' decision-making processes to stakeholders and beneficiaries.

3.   Bias and Fairness:

AI systems can perpetuate bias and inequality due to the data they are trained on. NPOs must be cautious when using AI data analysis to ensure ethical AI practices, including mitigating bias. They must also proactively identify and address potential biases in their data sets while promoting fairness and non-discrimination when using AI models without posing a disadvantage to any particular group. NPOs must ensure that their AI models are used fairly and equitably to avoid perpetuating inequalities.

4.   Impact Assessment and Risk Management

AI technology advances, organizations must conduct impact assessments and manage risks associated with AI applications.

Failure to deliver intended outcomes may require strategy adjustments. AI poses risks such as reputation harm from errors and security breaches from hackers targeting AI. Organizations should have contingency plans and safeguards in place to mitigate these risks. Responsible AI development and use also require prioritizing privacy, data protection, and human rights considerations. Organizations should prioritize these aspects when implementing AI applications.

5.   Consent for AI-driven Interventions:

In situations where AI is used to influence or make decisions that affect individuals directly, obtaining informed consent is a crucial ethical consideration, especially in personalized interventions, data collection, and other AI-driven initiatives. Non-profit organizations (NPOs) must prioritize transparency and ensure that individuals fully comprehend and agree to how AI is being employed in their interactions with the organization. This ensures that individuals have control over their data and can make informed decisions about their involvement in AI-driven initiatives.

6.   Encourage responsible AI usage within the nonprofit sector:

Actively promote ethical AI development and implementation throughout the entire nonprofit community. This involves minimizing potential harms and promoting transparency and accountability in AI decision-making processes. By championing responsible AI use, nonprofits can help ensure that AI is deployed to maximize its benefits while minimizing potential risks.

CHAPTER TEN

Building a Sustainable and Inclusive AI Ecosystem

D ata privacy, also known as information privacy, is a crucial aspect of data protection that focuses on the appropriate storage, access, retention, immutability, and security of sensitive data. It falls under the broader data protection umbrella, encompassing traditional data protection measures such as data backups, disaster recovery considerations, and data security. Data protection aims to preserve sensitive business data's confidentiality, integrity, and availability.

Data protection and privacy are often used interchangeably, but there is a significant difference between the two. Data privacy defines who has access to data, while data protection provides the tools and policies to restrict access to that data. Compliance laws help ensure that organizations implement user privacy requests, and it is the responsibility of these organizations to take measures to protect private user data.

Generally speaking, data privacy is commonly associated with properly handling personal data or personally identifiable information (PII), such as names, addresses, Social Security numbers, and credit card numbers. However, the concept extends to other valuable or confidential data, including financial information, intellectual property, and personal health information (PHI). In nonprofits, however, data privacy guidelines are based on the sensitivity and importance of data handling. It applies to all sensitive information organizations manage, including donors, sponsors, stakeholders, and employee information. This information is crucial to nonprofits' operations, development, and finances.

Data privacy helps ensure that sensitive data is accessible only to authorized parties. It prevents criminals from maliciously using this information and helps organizations meet regulatory requirements. Although the legal definition of data privacy varies by region, it generally refers to an individual's ability to determine what, when, and how their personal information is shared. This may include their name, contact information, current location, medical information, and purchase history.

In today's digital age, non-profit organizations rely heavily on data and technology to execute their missions efficiently. However, this also exposes them to various data privacy and security risks. Non-profits must prioritize data protection to preserve the trust of their donors, beneficiaries, and stakeholders. It is essential to know that various factors can cause cyber threats externally, such as hacking and malware attacks. Leaders of nonprofits must also recognize that unintentional data breaches can pose significant risks. Everyday business activities that can lead to data breaches and potential liability for organizations include conducting e-commerce on websites, storing and transferring personal data (both virtual and paper records), allowing partners and vendors to access personal information without proper safeguards, and storing personal information on laptops, smartphones, or cloud servers. These activities can result in the loss, theft, or unauthorized access to sensitive information, damaging an organization's reputation, eroding donor trust, and resulting in financial losses. Therefore, nonprofit leaders must prioritize data privacy and security measures to mitigate these risks.

Components of Data Privacy

Data privacy is a multifaceted concept that encompasses several key elements. These elements work together to ensure the appropriate handling and protection of sensitive data. The following are the six primary components of data privacy:

1. **Global Requirements**: Different legal jurisdictions worldwide may have different data privacy and compliance requirements. Organizations operating in multiple jurisdictions must be aware of these differences and ensure they meet all applicable requirements. For example, the General Data Protection Regulation (GDPR) applies to any organization processing personal data of EU residents, regardless of where that organization is based.

2. **Legal Framework**: Data privacy laws and regulatory requirements form the foundation of data privacy. These laws dictate how organizations must handle personal data, individuals' rights over their data, and non-compliance penalties. Examples of such laws include the GDPR in the European Union and the California Consumer Protection Act (CCPA) in California, USA.

3. **Third-party Associations:** Many organizations use third-party service providers like cloud or marketing agencies to handle their data. These third parties must also adhere to data privacy requirements, and organizations should ensure that they have appropriate contracts to govern these relationships.

4. **Policies:** Policies are internal business rules and guidelines that govern how an organization handles personal data. These policies should align with legal requirements and reflect the best data privacy and protection practices. Policies may cover data access, retention, destruction,

employee training, and awareness.

5. **Practices:** Practices refer to the day-to-day activities and procedures an organization follows to ensure data privacy. These practices should be based on policies and legal requirements and may include measures such as encryption, access controls, and regular security assessments.

6. **Data Governance:** Data governance refers to the standards and practices used to store, secure, retain, and access data. This includes data classification, backup and recovery procedures, and disaster recovery planning. Effective data governance helps ensure data is available when needed while protecting it from unauthorized access or misuse.

Considerations for Data Privacy and Security:

1. Develop a comprehensive data privacy and security policy: Non-profits should establish a detailed policy outlining their data privacy and security approach. This policy should cover all aspects of data handling, from collection and storage to access and disposal.

2. Conduct regular risk assessments: Non-profits should conduct regular risk assessments to identify potential threats to their data and systems. This will enable them to take proactive measures to mitigate these risks.

3. Implement strong access controls: Non-profits should implement strong access controls to ensure that only authorized personnel can access sensitive data. This includes the use of passwords, biometric authentication, and multi-factor authentication.

4. Encrypt sensitive data: Non-profits should encrypt all sensitive data in transit and at rest to prevent unauthorized access in case of a breach.

5. Regularly backup critical data: Non-profits should regularly

backup essential data to prevent data loss in a disaster or cyber-attack.

6.   Train staff on data privacy and security: Non-profits should provide regular training on data privacy and security best practices. This will ensure that everyone in the organization understands their responsibilities regarding data handling.

7.   Conduct regular security audits: Non-profits should conduct regular security audits to identify any weaknesses in their systems and address them promptly.

8.   Maintain open communication with stakeholders: Non-profits should maintain open communication with their donors, beneficiaries, and stakeholders regarding their data privacy and security approach. This will help build trust and transparency with these critical groups.

In summary, protecting the personal information of donors and other members is crucial for NPOs as it builds trust and prevents potential harm from data breaches. Failing to maintain data privacy and security can result in significant consequences, such as loss of resources, time, money, and reputation damage and eroding the faith of donors, volunteers, employees, and other stakeholders. Therefore, NPOs should prioritize data privacy and security measures to mitigate these risks.

PART FOUR:

BEYOND AI'S FOR NONPROFIT

CHAPTER ELEVEN

The Future of AI in Nonprofit Organizations

As artificial intelligence (AI) technology evolves, its impact on the nonprofit sector becomes increasingly apparent. The future of AI in nonprofits is promising, with the potential to revolutionize how these organizations operate and deliver their missions.

Here are a few things we can expect:

Deeper Insights: One of the most significant ways AI will impact nonprofits is by providing deeper insights into their operations and beneficiaries. By analyzing vast amounts of data, AI can uncover hidden patterns and trends that would be difficult or impossible for humans to identify. This information can help nonprofits make more informed decisions about resource allocation, program design, and fundraising strategies.

Enhanced Donor Engagement: Another area where AI will significantly impact is donor engagement. By using AI to analyze donor data, nonprofits can better understand their donors' preferences, behaviors, and motivations. This knowledge can be used to create more personalized and engaging experiences for donors, leading to stronger connections and greater loyalty.

Reduced Repetitive Tasks: AI can also automate repetitive tasks like data entry, scheduling appointments, and generating reports. This frees up valuable human resources to focus on higher-level tasks like program development and community engagement. By automating these tasks, nonprofits can reduce administrative overhead and allocate more resources to their core missions.

Improved Efficiency: Automating repetitive tasks will also enhance efficiency in nonprofit operations. By streamlining processes and reducing administrative burdens, nonprofits can operate more efficiently and effectively, leading to more significant impact and sustainability.

Data-Driven Decision Making: AI will provide nonprofits with valuable insights to help them make informed decisions about fundraising, program design, and resource allocation. By using data to inform decision-making, nonprofits can optimize their operations and maximize their impact.

Predictive Modeling: Another area where AI will significantly impact is predictive modeling. Using AI to analyze historical data, nonprofits can predict future trends and identify emerging needs. This knowledge can be used to develop innovative solutions ahead of the curve, which can help nonprofits stay ahead of the competition and deliver a more significant impact.

AI-Powered Fundraising: As AI technology becomes more advanced, it will become increasingly common for nonprofits to use AI-powered fundraising campaigns. These campaigns will use predictive analytics and AI tools to identify potential donors, personalize fundraising messages, and optimize fundraising strategies for maximum efficiency and sustainability.

Ethical AI: Nonprofits must prioritize moral AI development as they adopt these technologies. This means ensuring transparency, accountability, and fairness in data collection and algorithm design. By prioritizing these values, nonprofits can build trust with communities and donors, fostering long-term support and sustainability.

AI is poised to revolutionize the nonprofit sector by providing customized data solutions for nonprofit organizations as nonprofits can streamline their operations, engage donors more effectively, and significantly impact the causes they champion with its unique tools. As AI technology continues to advance, no doubt embracing this technology will better position nonprofits to succeed in a rapidly changing world.

CHAPTER TWELVE

Key Takeaways- Guiding
Nonprofit AI Initiatives

Nonprofit organizations operate for social or public benefit rather than profit and are governed by a board of directors or trustees. They face internal and external challenges, including governance, personnel, financial accountability, fundraising, operational issues, and changing donor preferences. Nonprofit initiatives aim to address social or environmental problems, promote social justice, assist needy people, raise awareness, inspire action, and build relationships. Nonprofit values include service, social justice, collaboration, transparency, and accountability. Effective nonprofit leadership styles include data and results-oriented, collaborative, mission-driven, strategic, adaptable, transparent and ethical, learning-oriented, transformational, charismatic, transactional, and participative. Collaboration is crucial for nonprofit success as it promotes increased accountability and transparency, efficient use of resources, new ideas, best practices, and lasting success through joint ventures, partnerships, and networks.

Integrating generations and artificial intelligence in nonprofit organizations presents opportunities and challenges. Each generation brings unique perspectives, values, and skills to the table, and recognizing these strengths can lead to effective collaboration and synergy. Nonprofits should develop AI initiatives responsibly and inclusively, addressing concerns about privacy, bias, and ethical implications and involving all generations in decision-making. Collaboration between individuals with diverse expertise can lead to cross-disciplinary innovation in AI initiatives that align with nonprofit missions. Nonprofits should foster open communication, respect for each other's perspectives, and a focus on responsible and inclusive AI development. Creating cross-generational teams that work together on AI initiatives can promote collaboration and shared ownership of projects. Nonprofits should invest in collaboration tools and technology that facilitate communication and knowledge sharing to promote intergenerational cooperation and collaboration across disciplines. Highlighting and recognizing collaborative leaders through awards, public acknowledgments, or other forms of recognition can inspire others to follow suit and contribute to the success of AI projects, reinforcing the importance of collaboration and encouraging others to adopt collaborative practices in their work.

In addition to these considerations related to AI and collaboration across generations, nonprofit organizations must also prioritize data privacy and security in their operations to protect the sensitive information of their donors, beneficiaries, employees, and other stakeholders. Nonprofits should conduct regular data privacy and security training for staff; implement strong data encryption standards; regularly test backup and recovery procedures; implement multi-factor authentication; regularly monitor network traffic; periodically review and update policies and procedures; conduct regular vulnerability assessments; implement strong access controls for third-party service providers; regularly test disaster recovery plans; and maintain open communication with stakeholders regarding data breaches, by prioritizing data privacy and security in their operations in these ways, as well as through collaboration across generations and responsible AI development practices, nonprofit organizations can better protect sensitive information while also advancing their missions in innovative ways through the use of AI technologies.

CONCLUSION

As the world becomes increasingly interconnected and complex, nonprofit organizations recognize the need to adopt new technologies to address pressing social and environmental challenges. Among these technologies, artificial intelligence (AI) is emerging as a game-changer, offering nonprofits unprecedented opportunities to improve their operations, enhance their impact, and better serve their beneficiaries.

This book, Pioneering Nonprofit AI Initiatives: A Guide to Generational Diversity, Ethics, and Collaboration, has explored how nonprofits can leverage AI to achieve their missions while revealing how AI can provide deeper insights into beneficiaries and programs, enhance donor engagement, automate repetitive tasks, improve efficiency, enable data-driven decision making, facilitate predictive modeling, and power AI-driven fundraising campaigns.

We have also acknowledged that adopting AI in nonprofit organizations is challenging. These challenges include generational divides in AI literacy and adoption, the need for ethical AI development and implementation, and the importance of collaboration between nonprofits, technology companies, and other stakeholders.

In conclusion, this book has sought to provide a roadmap for nonprofit organizations as they embark on their AI journeys by highlighting the benefits and challenges of AI adoption in nonprofits and offering practical guidance on how to navigate these issues while acknowledging the importance of generational diversity, ethics, and collaboration in driving successful AI initiatives.

By following these principles and embracing AI as a transformative force for good, nonprofit organizations can unlock new opportunities for impact and sustainability.

APPENDICES

Essential Definitions

In the world of nonprofit AI initiatives, it is essential to have a clear understanding of key terms and concepts. The following list provides definitions for some of the most vital terms discussed in this guide:

1. Artificial Intelligence (AI): AI refers to developing computer systems that can perform tasks that typically require human intelligence, such as visual perception, speech recognition, decision-making, and language translation.

2. Generational Diversity: Generational diversity encompasses the range of age groups present in an organization or society, such as Baby Boomers, Generation X, Millennials, and Generation Z. Understanding and leveraging the unique perspectives of each generation is essential for effective nonprofit AI initiatives.

3. Mission-Driven: Mission-driven organizations are nonprofits with a clear mission or purpose guiding their activities and decision-making. The task is central to the organization's existence and goals.

4.   Ethical AI: Ethical AI involves the development and use of artificial intelligence in ways that align with moral principles, fairness, transparency, and social responsibility. It prioritizes ethical decision-making in AI systems.

5.   Data Privacy: Data privacy protects personal and sensitive information from unauthorized access, use, or disclosure. It includes measures to ensure data security and compliance with relevant privacy regulations.

6.   Compliance: Compliance relates to laws, regulations, and standards governing data privacy, ethical practices, or other relevant aspects of AI initiatives. Nonprofit organizations must maintain legal and ethical compliance.

7.   Adaptability: Adaptability is the capacity to adjust and respond effectively to change, particularly in the face of technological advancements, uncertainties, and unexpected challenges.

8.   Resilience: Resilience involves the ability to bounce back and recover from setbacks, adversity, or unforeseen circumstances. Resilient organizations can weather challenges and adapt to changing conditions.

9.   Collaboration: Collaboration is working with individuals from diverse backgrounds and expertise to achieve common goals. It often involves teamwork and knowledge sharing.

10.   Cross-Generational   Mentorship: Cross-generational

mentorship is a mentoring relationship in which individuals from different generations learn from each other, transferring knowledge, skills, and insights across age groups.

11.   Agile Implementation: Agile implementation is a project management methodology focusing on flexibility, adaptability, and iterative progress. It allows organizations to respond quickly to changes and challenges.

12.   Data Minimization: Data minimization collects and stores only the minimum amount necessary for a specific purpose. It helps reduce the risks associated with data privacy and security.

13.   Anonymization: Anonymization removes or alters personal identifiers from data to protect individual privacy. It ensures that data cannot be linked to specific individuals.

14.   Scenario Planning: Scenario planning involves developing and analyzing potential future scenarios to prepare for different outcomes and make informed decisions based on these scenarios.

15.   Crisis Response Protocols: Crisis response protocols are pre-established plans and procedures that organizations follow when faced with unexpected crises or emergencies. They aim to ensure a coordinated and effective response to challenges.

These definitions are a foundation for understanding the concepts and principles discussed throughout this guide. A shared understanding of these key terms is vital for effective communication and collaboration in nonprofit AI initiatives.

REFERENCES

Bigelow, S. J. (2022, August 9). Data *privacy (information privacy)*. CIO. https://www.techtarget.com/searchcio/definition/data-privacy-information-privacy

Colquitt, J. A., LePine, J. A., & Noe, R. A. (2000). Toward an integrative theory of training motivation: A meta-analytic path analysis of 20 years of research. Journal of Applied Psychology, 85(5), 678–707.

Cook, S., Yates, J., & O'Brien, J. (2010). Influences on corporate social responsibility for small and medium-sized contractors. Journal of Construction Engineering and Management (,.

Copeland, B. (2023, December 14). *Artificial intelligence (AI) | Definition, Examples, Types, Applications, Companies, & Facts.* Encyclopedia Britannica. https://www.britannica.com/technology/artificial-intelligence

Cox, T. (1994). Cultural diversity in organizations: Theory, research, and practice. Berrett-Koehler.

Data Privacy and Cyber Liability: What You Do not Know Puts Your Mission at Risk – Nonprofit Risk Management Center. (2019, October 16). Nonprofit Risk Management Center. https://nonprofitrisk.org/resources/articles/data-privacy-and-cyber-liability-what-you-dont-know-puts-your-mission-at-risk/

DeRue, D. S., Nahrgang, J. D., Wellman, N., & Dienesch, R. M. (2011). Leadership and motivation: The practical application of expectancy theory. Journal of Applied Psychology, 96(4), 690-701.

Eby, L. T., Allen, T. D., Evans, S. C., Ng, T., & DuBois, D. L. (2013). Does mentoring matter? A multidisciplinary meta-analysis comparing mentored and non-mentored individuals. Journal of Vocational Behavior, 83(3), 1-15.

F. (2021, August 23). 7 Major Benefits of Nonprofit Collaboration. Firespring. https://firespring.com/solutions-for-nonprofits/7-major-benefits-of-nonprofit-collaboration/

H. (2023, September 20). *The Future of AI and its Impact on Nonprofits - Humanata - Medium.* Medium. https://medium.com/@humanata/the-future-of-ai-and-its-impact-on-nonprofits-385ca7ed869b

Hanna, K. T. (2022, June 9). Nonprofit organization (NPO). WhatIs. https://www.techtarget.com/whatis/definition/non-profit-organization-NPO

Holt, M. (n.d.). *Artificial Intelligence in Modern Society.* Murray State's Digital Commons. https://digitalcommons.murraystate.edu/bis437/138/?utm_source=digitalcommons.murraystate.edu%2Fbis437%2F138&utm_medium=PDF&utm_campaign=PDFCoverPages

Hong, L., & Page, S. E. (2004). Groups of diverse problem solvers can outperform groups of high-ability problem solvers. Proceedings of the National Academy of Sciences, 101(46), 16385–16389.

Kenton, W. (2023, December 3). Nonprofit Organization (NPO): Definition and Example. Investopedia. https://www.investopedia.com/terms/n/non-profitorganization.asp

Kotter, J. P. (1996). Leading change. Harvard Business Review, 74(2), 96-103.

Launching a Nonprofit Initiative? Here is Everything You Must Know. (n.d.). https://www.softwareadvice.com/resources/nonprofit-initiative/

Noe, R. A. (1988). An investigation of the determinants of successful assigned mentoring relationships. Personnel Psycholog, (3), pp. 457–479.

Nonprofit Impact Matters. (n.d.). Nonprofit Impact Matters. https://www.nonprofitimpactmatters.org/?utm_source=web&utm_medium=site&utm_campaign=reports-page

Nonprofits, A. F. (2023, November 29). *Navigating the Ethical Landscape: AI in Nonprofit Organizations.* Medium. https://

medium.com/@aifornonprofits/navigating-the-ethical-landscape-ai-in-nonprofit-organizations-4247c2cb6718

Page, S. E. (2007). Making the difference: Applying a logic of diversity. Academy of Management Perspective, (4), pp. 6–20.

Sessa, V. I., Kabacoff, R. I., Deal, J. J., & Brown, H. (2007, January 1). *Generational differences in leader values and leadership behaviors.* The Psychologist-Manager Journal. https://doi.org/10.1080/10887150709336612

Skiles, M. (2023, December 8). *AI for Nonprofits: How to Use Artificial Intelligence for Good | Nonprofit Blog.* Nonprofit Blog. https://donorbox.org/nonprofit-blog/ai-for-nonprofits

Team, D. I. (2023, December 11). *AI For Nonprofits: Everything Your Org Needs to Know | DonorSearch.* DonorSearch. https://www.donorsearch.net/resources/ai-for-nonprofits/

Van Ginkel, W. P., Van Knippenberg, D., & Dreu, C. K. W. D. (2000). Interdependence in multiteam systems: The effect of subunit interdependence on multiteam system behavior. Journal of Applied Psychology, 85(2), 204–218.

Vail, K. (2023, October 16). *AI and Nonprofits: What Boards Need to Know.* BoardEffect. https://www.boardeffect.com/blog/ai-and-nonprofits-what-boards-need-to-know/#:~:text=AI%20relies%20heavily%20on%20data,and%20while%20maintaining%20donor%20trust

Vijal. (1970, October 27). *27 OCT common challenges that businesses face in AI adoption and how to overcome them.* Common challenges that businesses face in AI adoption and how to overcome them. https://nuvento.com/blog/common-challenges-that-businesses-face-in-ai-adoption-and-how-to-overcome-them/

What kind of leader are you? Five leadership styles for non-profits | Central Michigan University. (n.d.). www.cmich.edu. https://www.cmich.edu/blog/all-things-higher-ed/five-leadership-styles-for-non-profits

What is Data Protection and Privacy? (2023, October 27).

Cloudian. https://cloudian.com/guides/data-protection/data-protection-and-privacy-7-ways-to-protect-user-data/

What is a "Nonprofit"? (n.d.). National Council of Nonprofits. https://www.councilofnonprofits.org/what-nonprofit

Wong, G. K., & Roy, M. M. (2016). Effects of team collaboration on innovation in entrepreneurial ventures. The Journal of High Technology Management Research, 27(1), 1-14.

York, A. (2023, November 9). *10 Must-Try AI Tools for Nonprofits in 2023*. ClickUp. https://clickup.com/blog/ai-tools-for-nonprofits/#:~:text=Looka-,What%20Are%20AI%20Tools%20for%20Nonprofits%3F,engagement%20and%20analyze%20donor%20data.